AO/IB   42e-

D0186188

GLASS FROM WORLD'S FAIRS

1851 – 1904

JANE SHADEL SPILLMAN

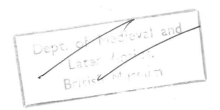

THE CORNING MUSEUM OF GLASS

CORNING, NEW YORK

1986

Cover design from *L'Exposition de Paris, 1889. Journal hebdomadaire.*
Endpapers: The Glass Works of Gillinder & Sons at the Philadelphia
   Centennial, from *Frank Leslie's Illustrated Newspaper.*
Frontispiece: The Crystal Palace from a contemporary print, 1851.
Copyright © 1986
The Corning Museum of Glass
Corning, New York 14831
Printed in West Germany by Philipp von Zabern, Mainz
Standard Book Numbers
ISBN 0-87290-113-0 (hardcover) · ISBN 0-87290-114-9 (softcover)
Library of Congress Catalog Card Number 85-73656
Photography: Raymond F. Errett and Nicholas L. Williams except as noted.
Editor: Richard W. Price

GLASS FROM WORLD'S FAIRS
1851 – 1904

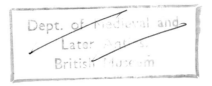

Table of Contents

Introduction

How many visitors to Expo 67 in Montreal or the 1984 Louisiana World Exposition in New Orleans realized that, behind the futuristic trappings, these great spectacles were survivals from the Victorian era? The first world's fair was the Great Exhibition of the Works of Industry of All Nations, held in London's Crystal Palace during the summer of 1851. The popular name for that and succeeding exhibitions was coined by Thackeray's Irishman Mr. Molony, who gazed in awe at the multitude of displays in the Crystal Palace and said:

> With conscious proide
> I stud insoide
> And look'd the World's Great Fair in
> Until me sight
> Was dazzled quite
> And couldn't see for staring.

The world's fairs of the 19th century were an outgrowth of tremendous changes in society. The technological innovations of the Industrial Revolution brought masses of workers from the country to the city factories. These factories created thousands of products which demanded an international market, and the growth of the railways enabled the goods to be shipped to market more efficiently than by water transport or horse-drawn cart. As the middle class rapidly increased in numbers and prosperity, more people received more education and had more time and money to visit exhibitions. Without this combination of factors, it is doubtful that world's fairs would have been successful. In earlier times only a limited number of people would have had the interest or the means to visit an exposition, and the problems of transporting many exhibits over great distances would have been insurmountable.

There were 58 international expositions between 1851 and World War I, but those held in non-industrialized nations far from major population centers had little chance of attracting enough exhibits or viewers to succeed financially. As world's fairs became more popular and competition among host countries grew more intense, the Bureau des Expositions in Paris was created by international treaty in 1931 to see that these events were not staged too close geographically or too frequently.

In England and the United States, private interests sponsored the exhibitions; in France, the national government provided the financing and administration. In either case, there was a determined attempt by the host country to outdo previous fairs in acreage, number of exhibits, beauty of displays, and technological innovations. The fairs offered an irresistible opportunity to celebrate progress in the realms of technology, manufacturing, and the fine arts.

Because international expositions were important to national pride, many governments encouraged manufacturers to send displays by underwriting some of the transportation costs. Established firms participated because it was prestigious to do so; newer, smaller companies designed exhibits in the hope of opening new markets. Businessmen offered their newest, largest, and best products and hoped to sell most of them. Some very large or complex objects, created just for display at the fairs, often remained unsold to decorate the factory showrooms. Most of the objects, however, were goods from sellers' regular lines; when one item was purchased by a visitor, it was replaced by another.

The fairs were called "universal exhibitions" because they presented displays of natural history and fine arts as well as manufactures. While new inventions were promoted by the industrialized nations, ethnic products and raw materials were featured by colonies and territories which were not yet capable of mass production. This variety of exhibits was part of a plan to organize and display all of man's knowledge in one place. The American painter and inventor Samuel Morse thought his children could learn more from five weeks at the 1867 Paris fair than from five years of travel or study.

In addition to their commercial and educational functions, the expositions pioneered a form of mass entertainment. A visit to the fair was the 19th-century equivalent of a trip to Disney World. Many things which we now take for granted were first seen at one of the exhibitions. Thomas Cook, for example, made a fortune selling special rail excursion tickets which included an admission to the Crystal Palace; he went on to develop the package tour. Both the Ferris wheel and the honky-tonk Midway of American county fairs were born in Chicago in 1893; the ice cream cone was created at the St. Louis fair on a hot day in 1904.

As the exhibitions increased in popularity, they also grew in size. The London fair of 1851 was housed in one building and attracted six million visitors. Attendance swelled to 48 million at the 1900 exposition, and the St. Louis fair covered 1,300 acres. To help visitors cover the longer distances, some fairs used boats and others tried moving sidewalks or other forms of electric transportation. The efficient handling of crowds at modern sports events and rock concerts was developed by the planners of world's fairs.

More tangible legacies of these events are the museum buildings and collections which they financed. The Victoria & Albert Museum in London, the art museums in Glasgow and St. Louis, the science museum in Chicago, and the Trocadero, Grand and Petit Palaces, and Eiffel Tower in Paris were all created for, or financed by, an international exhibition.

There were 11 "major" world's fairs between 1851 and 1904. They attracted the largest numbers of exhibits, foreign participants, and visitors. Although several of these expositions lost money, all were successful in their primary goals: showing the assembled displays to millions of visitors and added prestige for the host nation.

The glass exhibits of these 11 fairs were large, and in studying them it is possible to see a progression of styles. Each fair is a time capsule featuring what was most admired in a given year. The 19th-century art movements affecting glass culminated in the free-form glass of Art Nouveau and the rigidity of American brilliant-cut glass, two radically different styles both at the peak of popularity around 1900. After 1904, glass design entered a period of stagnation from which it did not emerge until the triumphant exhibit of modern decorative arts in Paris in 1925.

1851, London

The Great Exhibition of the Works of Industry of All Nations was opened by Queen Victoria in Hyde Park on May 1, 1851. Gaily costumed representatives of foreign nations and British possessions attended the opening and praised the displays. The number and breadth of the exhibits and the remarkable Crystal Palace — the glass building which housed them all — were staggering in their effect. The British press was ecstatic, and visitors flocked to see the magnificent building and its contents. They found, under one roof, 26 acres of displays and nearly 14,000 separate exhibits of natural history and manufactured goods.

The building made architectural and engineering history. It was designed by Joseph Paxton, estate manager and one-time gardener to the duke of Devonshire. Paxton had designed greenhouses, but no glass structure on the scale of this one had been conceived before, much less erected. The building was nicknamed the "Crystal Palace" by *Punch* magazine and, to everyone's astonishment, it was completed in just 17 weeks! The modular construction of iron, glass, and wood was revolutionary, and it even rose high enough in its central section to enclose the row of elm trees which the London public had demanded be saved. During construction, there had been widespread fear that the glass building would blow over in

a high wind or collapse of its own weight. Once it was open, however, its obvious stability reassured the public.

The exhibition itself was the brainchild of Henry Cole, then a minor civil servant but later the first director of the Victoria & Albert Museum in London. With the backing of the prince consort, Cole directed the planning of an exhibition in which all nations of the world would be invited to participate. Prince Albert hoped to promote world peace and to raise the artistic level of English products by showing manufacturers and craftsmen what other countries had accomplished. About half of the exhibition space was allotted to England and half to other countries. Along with displays of textiles, furniture, metals, and ceramics, a wide variety of glassware was shown.

In the center of the Crystal Palace stood the most stunning glass exhibit of all: the Crystal Fountain. The fountain, 27 feet high, was the creation of F. & C. Osler of Birmingham. The iron piping and supports were completely hidden by the molded and cut sections of glass, and the shimmering mass of falling water and crystal facets amazed visitors.

Because the exhibition was in England, British glassmakers predominated; however, many Continental glass manufacturers and two American firms were among the 157 glass exhibitors. Displays of flat glass, bottles, and other everyday products of the glass industry competed with tableware for the attention of viewers.

Most of the English glass shown at the fair was the traditional colorless lead glass which had been popu-

◁ Fig. 1. The Crystal Fountain, from "Interior of the Great Exhibition, No. 2, North Transept," engraved for *Mighty London Illustrated.*

lar for a century and a half. It was cut, engraved, and sometimes fancifully shaped. There were some examples of opaque white or colored wares, with enameled (painted and fired) decoration based on classical mythology. Two English factories displayed the new technique of glass pressing in the form of small busts of Queen Victoria, Prince Albert, and other notables. A few glasshouses showed the colored, cut, engraved, and gilded glass which had been recently introduced, from Bohemia.

Twenty-six glass manufacturers from the Austro-Hungarian Empire, the majority with factories in Bohemia, dazzled visitors with hundreds of richly colored objects. Hoffman of Prague, Count Harrach of Neuwelt, and others each sent 100 or more objects; most of these were sold and remained in England. They included vases of alabaster, hyalith, ruby, and several shades of blue and green glass. Harrach's prize-winning exhibit included overlay glasses, cut and engraved glass, and vases decorated with gilt scrolls. The classical influence so noticeable in the English glass was not present in the elaborately decorated Bohemian glassware.

Other countries presented smaller displays. The Venetian glass industry was at the beginning of its 19th-century revival, and the Venetian manufacturer Pietro Bigaglia sent a display of glass beads, paperweights, cigar holders, and a mosaic picture.

Even before the exhibition, Bohemian and Venetian glassmakers were exerting an influence on English glass. Both "Anglo-Venetian" glass and layered, cut, and engraved "Bohemian glass" in ruby, white, green, and blue were shown by English glassmakers along with their conservatively cut tablewares.

The French glass exhibits drew no particular acclaim from the critics. Baccarat and St. Louis, the largest French tableware factories, declined to participate. Anglo-French competitive feeling was still intense, and, since tariffs protected their markets, the French could afford to stand above the undignified pursuit of customers. M. Maës of Clichy-la-Garenne, a French maker of tableware, exhibited millefiori scent bottles and paperweights; the firm also won a medal for a new glass composition.

One American tableware manufacturer, John L. Gilliland of the Brooklyn Flint Glass Works, went to the considerable trouble and expense of participating. The purity of his glass, commended by several critics and the jury, is said to have impressed some English companies so much that they began to import American sand. The jurors awarded the Brooklyn firm a Prize Medal for flint glass.

Critics at the *Art-Journal,* an influential publication, praised both the English and the Bohemian manufacturers, citing the purity of the English glass and observing that Hoffman's glass was above the "gaudy vulgarities" usually associated with Bohemian glass.

In hindsight, it is evident that little innovative work was shown at the Great Exhibition. The glass, like many of the decorative arts displayed there, demonstrated the mid-19th-century love of decoration which was usually unrelated to the form or function of the object it adorned. However, it is a perfect microcosm of what Queen Victoria and her subjects considered "the best taste" in 1851. The principal reason the Royal Society of Arts backed the exposition was to raise the artistic level of British "art manufactures" or decorative arts. The exhibition was seen as a way to educate and inspire both the craftsmen and their customers by showing them the best that the world could offer. Part of the profit from the fair was used to found the South Kensington Museum (now the Victoria & Albert Museum) as a museum of design with a school of art.

Although it was originally intended to be a temporary structure, the Crystal Palace was so popular that it was preserved. The building and the Crystal Fountain were dismantled at the close of the exhibition and reerected at Sydenham on the southern outskirts of London. There they continued to amaze and delight visitors until they were destroyed by a spectacular fire in 1936.

Fig. 2. "Group of Glass by Count Harrach of Bohemia," pl. ▷ 38, *Industrial Arts of the Nineteenth Century at the Great Exhibition* by M. Digby Wyatt.

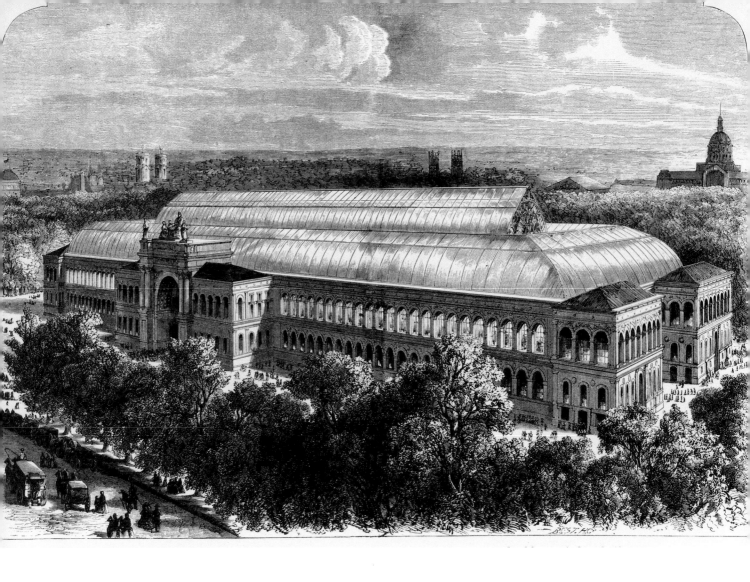

Fig. 3.   The Palais de l'Industrie, built for the Paris fair of 1855,
from *L'Illustration, Journal Universal.*

1855, Paris

The emperor Napoleon III regarded the Crystal Palace as the opening shot in a battle of one-upmanship. Accordingly, he planned his own world's fair for 1855. France was the wealthiest nation in Europe, with a population three times that of England, and the emperor was determined to equal or surpass the English achievement. He appointed his cousin, Prince Napoleon, to be chief administrator, and the prince was given an ample budget.

The 34-acre exposition site included the Palais de l'Industrie (a permanent building) to house the manufactured goods, the Palais des Beaux-Arts, and the Galerie des Machines. Fine arts had not been shown in London, where the emphasis was on art manufactures, and the French thought them to be a vital addition. Although the impact of the fair was diminished somewhat by dividing its 21,000 displays among three buildings, it attracted more than five million visitors during the six months it was open. The fair produced no profit, but the emperor was satisfied with the results. The crowning moment was the arrival of Queen Victoria and Prince Albert to visit the imperial family and tour the exposition. It marked the first visit to France by an English monarch since Henry VIII met Francis I on the Field of the Cloth of Gold in 1520.

There were fewer glass exhibits in Paris than there had been in London, but the displays were still imposing. About half of the nearly 140 glassmakers were French. The exhibitors from the host nation outdid themselves. Most of them had not provided displays for the London fair, and national pride demanded that they show off this time. The exhibits of Baccarat, Clichy, and St. Louis were highly praised. Fortunately, Baccarat preserved a detailed, handwritten list of the several hundred objects that firm presented. Most were table services in cut or engraved glass, but some were "objets de fantasie," a category which included glasses with Venetian-type threading and bright colors. Baccarat also showed two candelabra, each about 18 feet tall, which compared favorably with the 30-foot-tall gas candelabrum sent by Osler. The critics lauded St. Louis's vases which imitated Bohemian crystal and Clichy's blue vases for their perfect imitation of Sèvres porcelain. Clichy also displayed transparent ruby red glass. Although no paperweights are mentioned by reporters, the Baccarat list includes several, and it is likely that Clichy and St. Louis showed them too.

The factory of Monot et Cie. at La Villette, France, sent a pair of 24-inch white vases enameled and gilded in a floral design. These are similar to French porcelain of the period, and they won admiring comments from the press.

One remarkable French exhibit was a life-sized lion and serpent made entirely of glass fibers by an artist named Lambourg, now in the collection of the Conservatoire des Arts et Métiers in Paris. Hats, wigs, dolls, and dresses of glass fibers appeared at later fairs, but these objects, like the lion, were novelties which had little practical use. It was not until the 20th century that the manufacture and utilization of glass fibers became commercially feasible.

The German and Bohemian glass at Paris was apparently similar to that shown in London in 1851.

The Bavarian glass dealer F. Steigerwald of Munich offered an array of colored, cut, and engraved glass which so impressed the South Kensington Museum that several pieces were purchased for its collection.

Except for the large candelabrum sent by F. & C. Osler, there was little British glass in evidence. The *Art-Journal* complained that the English manufacturers had neglected their duty by failing to send exhibits to Paris. It is not clear whether English glassmakers thought the effort was not worth the expense since the French glass market was protected by high tariffs or whether Anglo-French rivalry caused them to stay home.

Contemporary illustrations of the glass shown in Paris are hard to find, but reports indicate that it must have been similar in style to that shown in London four years earlier. The general comment about the Bohemian glass was that it was ''as usual.'' The superior qualities of the English and French lead glass were hotly debated; the national origin of the writer seemed to exercise a greater bearing on his opinion than any actual merits of the glass. It was not until the next international exhibition, held in London in 1862, that real stylistic progress could be seen.

Fig. 4. Pair of opaque white vases in ''Medici shape'' with ▷ enameled and gilt decoration. Made by Monot et Cie., La Villette, France, for exhibition at the Paris fair of 1855. H. 69.5 cm. Collection of the Musée National des Techniques — CNAM, Paris. (Inv. No. 14006$^{1}/_{2}$; gift of Monot family in 1906.)

Fig. 5. Watercolor by E. S. Cole, ''Official Opening of the 1862
Exhibition.'' Collection of the Victoria & Albert Museum, London.

16

1862, London

Inspired by the resounding success of the Crystal Palace exposition, the Royal Society of Arts determined to repeat the event. Perhaps because the 1851 building was still in existence and because the organizers were trying to be different, they chose a solid, conservative design which was universally condemned by the press as ugly. Despite the criticism, the structure was erected on Cromwell Road. It was demolished, as planned, after the close of the fair.

There were more foreign exhibitors than in 1851. Again, American industry was underrepresented, but for a good reason: the United States government, in the middle of the Civil War, had neither appointed an official commission to the fair nor urged manufacturers to take part. Prince Albert's death a few months before the exhibition opened also put a damper on the proceedings. Queen Victoria had attended and delighted in the Crystal Palace exhibition again and again, but Albert's death occupied her thoughts to the exclusion of almost everything else, and she was less interested in the second London fair.

Glass was shown by 202 exhibitors, of whom 80 were British. The British press took great pride in their display. The *Art-Journal* text on glass complacently begins:

> The position of England in this section of the Exhibition presents a marked contrast to what is seen in several others. Here we stand, not only relatively first in the rate of progress, but absolutely first, both in quality of material and artistic development. . . . Workers in glass might, like workers in wood or metal, have based their forms upon the style of Louis XIV, or on the most vicious types of the later Renaissance. . . . Fortunately our glass manufacturers . . . founding the revival of their art upon the forms of Greece . . . have made the glass work of the English section the admiration of competing nations.

J. Defries and Sons, a specialist in lighting, and F. & C. Osler both presented displays distinguished more for weight than for artistic quality. Osler displayed again the 30-foot gas candelabrum which the firm had sent to Paris in 1855. Defries sent a slightly smaller one, several mammoth chandeliers, and a two-ton mirror made of prisms which had been created for the palace of the sultan of Turkey. These were objects of awe to the general public but they were hardly typical of British glass.

Another atypical but attention-getting display was the Morrison Tazza in the stand of Dobson & Pearce, a London decorating firm. This tazza had an elaborately engraved bowl rimmed with turquoise set in gold, as well as a gold base. The *Times* declared it to be "the most extraordinary specimen of art manufacture of its kind in the whole Exhibition." The tazza, only 12 inches high, was purchased during the first week of the fair for 250 guineas, then the largest sum ever paid for a piece of contemporary glass. Although the gold mounting undoubtedly added to the price, the object was judged as a work of art, not as glass tableware. Unfortunately, the tazza has not been recorded since the exhibition closed. It was an experi-

Fig. 6a. "Engraved and Coloured Glass by Messrs. W. P., & G. Phillips, London," pl. 68, from *Masterpieces of Industrial Art & Sculpture at the International Exhibition, 1862* by J. B. Waring.

ment that was not repeated; gold and gems generally were not regarded as suitable for glass decoration except perhaps in an ostentatious society such as the court of czarist Russia.

The heavy cut glass so prominent in 1851 was less evident in 1862. Engraved glasses were present in large numbers, accompanied by delicate Venetian-style glass with applied decoration which was shown by nearly all of the British exhibitors. Although no one would have mistaken these for Venetian pieces, the forms and decoration were obviously inspired by the fragile Italian objects. Along with their "Venetian" glass, W. P., & G. Phillips showed a three-foot glass table, the first of several examples of glass furniture which were to become a feature of later fairs. No pressed glass was shown; not even the novelties from 1851 were repeated. Pressed glass still was not a major product of the British glass industry, and it was not prestigious enough for display.

As in 1851, Baccarat and St. Louis declined to exhibit, but Maës of Clichy sent a well-filled stand. Felix Slade, a prominent London art collector, purchased a tazza from Clichy because he regarded it as one of the finest examples of engraving in the exposition. It differs very little from English engraving except that it is rather more abstract in design. The tazza is now in the British Museum.

The Bohemian glass, which had been so much admired in 1851, was not markedly different in 1862; it received little attention from the critics. The exhibition, however, did mark the international debut of J. & L. Lobmeyr of Vienna. Their delicately engraved glass provided a contrast to the standard colorful Bohemian wares and won praise from the press.

The British were convinced that the fair had achieved its purpose of demonstrating the higher level of taste and craftsmanship achieved by British industry, especially ''art manufactures,'' since 1851. Today, we can see that exhibitors such as Defries and Osler were preoccupied with impressive size; considerations of ''art'' seem to have been secondary for them. The Bohemian influence so evident on British glass in 1851 was completely absent. Classical influence was dominant in the subjects chosen for engraving by the British firms, but it was joined by Venetian, Moorish, medieval, and other romantic revival styles. The Venetian designs shown in 1862 were popular until the end of the decade, but they were out of favor by the 1870s. M. Maës and J. & L. Lobmeyr, both of whom seemed to be style leaders in 1862, displayed glass similar to the British entries, but other Bohemian glass companies were still making the brightly colored glasses which had been their mainstay for years.

Fig. 6 b. ''Specimens of Engraved Glass by Messrs. Dobson & Pearce, London,'' pl. 78, in *Masterpieces of Industrial Art & Sculpture at the International Exhibition, 1862.* The Morrison Tazza is shown in two views on the bottom row.

Fig. 7.   The main building for the Paris fair of 1867, from a contemporary lithograph, 1867. Courtesy Bibliothèque Nationale,
Paris.

1867, Paris

The bills had scarcely been paid from the second London exhibition when the emperor Napoleon III announced that France's second international exposition would be held in Paris in 1867. This was the largest fair to date. A mere increase in size, however, was not sufficient; the French added many features to make the exhibition more enjoyable for the average visitor, including national pavilions, restaurants, and an amusement park.

The principal exhibits were housed in a gigantic oval building designed by A. Gustave Eiffel, who was just beginning his engineering and architectural career. Displays were arranged in concentric circles around a central garden. Giant elevators carried visitors to the top of the iron structure for a panorama of the surrounding gardens. Each participating country had also been invited to erect a small pavilion; the result was more than a hundred lesser buildings dotting the Champs de Mars with a whimsical mixture of architectural styles. Contrary to all expectations, the fair opened on time, with most of the exhibits in place. It drew nearly seven million visitors, and, after the exposition had closed, the buildings were dismantled as planned.

Glass was displayed with furniture and other domestic objects. George Wallis of the South Kensington Museum, who wrote the article on glass for the *Art-Journal Catalogue* of the exhibition, reported, "The first glance at the French display, as a whole, produces some astonishment at the immense variety of coloured, gilded, and painted objects, brought together as glass." Wallis was critical of the French forms,

noting that they contradicted the nature of the material and were stiff, ornate, and better suited to an opaque material than to a transparent one.

Baccarat had the largest glass exhibit, and Wallis thought it was the best of the French displays: "The table glass, especially the cut specimens, are decidedly the best among the French. The forms are generally excellent, and in a pure style, while the arrangement of the ornamentation . . . gives a variety of light and shadow . . . rarely seen in cut glass. . . ." The official French illustrated publication mentioned Baccarat's monumental fountain, which was more than 20 feet high, engraved table glass, and glass in green, purple, yellow, blue, and opaque white. Wallis particularly praised a magnificent punch set created by Baccarat for the exposition. This was of colorless glass overlaid with blue, and the blue glass was acid-etched in a design showing Bacchus and his attendants. Wallis was struck by the delicacy of the acid etching, which was a new technique at the time. Several shadings of color were achieved by removing different amounts of the outer blue layer.

Colored glass was also the principal exhibit of the glassworks at Clichy, Pantin, and St. Louis. William P. Blake, one of the American commissioners, was particularly impressed by St. Louis's 20-foot-tall candelabrum.

American glassmakers were not yet convinced that the expense of exhibiting was justified by the new customers they might gain. However, one Pittsburgh glass manufacturer displayed pressed glass which found favor with a visiting British craftsman, if no one else:

> J. B. Lyon and Co., Pittsburg, U.S. exhibit articles in moulded glass superior to any I have ever seen. It is impossible to detect the marks of the mould. The wine-glasses are as thin at top as if made by hand, showing that it is possible, by careful manipulation in pressing to make moulded glass equally fine as by handwork.

Several Italian manufacturers exhibited glass, but the one mentioned in all of the contemporary accounts is Antonio Salviati. His mosaics and revivals of earlier Venetian work won great acclaim. Although Salviati's glass was considered impractical for daily use, most viewers were impressed by the fanciful forms and the skill with which they were executed. Wallis reported that the "glories of the Venetian glass of the 14th and 15th centuries" had been revived. *Art-Journal* illustrations show snake-stem goblets, some with applied threading, a large chandelier of colorless and colored glass with applied flowers and threading, and a mosaic.

J. & L. Lobmeyr was the only Austrian firm to receive much praise from the critics. The *Art-Journal* wrote that Lobmeyr's glasses were "unsurpassed by those of any other country" and illustrated the glass on five pages, more than the number allotted to any other glassmaker:

> The merit . . . is derived from superiority in forms and engraving; in the value of the actual metal he may be surpassed by other countries; but his works are conspicuous for high character in art, not only in reference to such as are elegancies, but such as are articles of daily use.

Most of the glasses illustrated are combinations of glass and ormolu. The British craftsman W. T. Swene commented, "The engraving in the Austrian court . . . was generally inferior to that of French manufacture, the only noteworthy examples being those of Herr Lobmeyr, of Vienna, whose Greek and medieval services were the best examples of engraving to be found in this section. . . ."

As in 1855, the British exhibits were small compared to the quantities of French and Bohemian glass shown. None of them was remarkable, although the engraved glass of Powell & Sons was commended for its absolute clarity. Engraved glass and Venetian-style glass filled most of the British stand. J. Defries and Sons of London showed a "Crystall Jewelled Candelabrum" which was 18 feet high, with 48 lights. Although the British critics defended the candelabrum as a wonderful example of the purity and sparkle of good British lead crystal, there were no compliments on the merits of the design, which seems singularly ugly today.

Baccarat was awarded a Grand Prize, while gold medals went to several other French factories. British glassmakers had to be content with silver medals.

No new styles or techniques in glassmaking were visible at this fair, which seemed like a second showing of the London fair of 1862. The French glass was traditional, although the Baccarat and St. Louis factories were obviously far more interested in colored glass than were their English competitors. The glass of Salviati, which reproduced styles of earlier centuries, took the Venetian revival a step further by presenting a variety of fanciful vessels in addition to mosaic and millefiori work, but his work was hardly original.

Creativity was apparently at a low ebb — but it burst forth with renewed vigor in the next decade.

Fig. 8. Punch set exhibited by the Cristalleries de Baccarat at ▷ the Paris fair of 1867. H. 56.5 cm. The Corning Museum of Glass (gift of Mrs. Charles K. Davis).

Fig. 9. The Palace of Industry, Vienna, 1873, from the *Art-Journal*, 1873.

1873, Vienna

Three international exhibitions were planned for the 1870s. The close proximity of these fairs guaranteed that the manufactures shown would be similar and increased the competitive nature of the expositions.

The imperial government of Austria was determined to host in 1873 an exhibition every bit as impressive as those already held in London and Paris. The emperor had been busy transforming his capital, Vienna, from a walled medieval town into a gracious 19th-century city, and he was anxious to show off the glories of the Prater (a large park by the Danube), the Ring (the boulevard where the city walls had been), the Opera House, and other imposing new structures he had created.

The exposition was held in the Prater, and several buildings were erected to house it. These were designed, very sensibly, so that they could continue to be used after the close of the fair. The main building was a huge structure known as the Palace of Industry. It was surmounted by a dome more than 350 feet in diameter, which was topped with a gigantic gilded, glass-jeweled replica of the imperial crown of Austria. There were separate, smaller buildings for machinery, fine arts, and agriculture. As at Paris in 1867, the park was filled with small structures erected by the countries participating in the exhibition. The displays numbered more than 25,000 — fewer than at the Paris fair, but more than at any other exposition.

It was reported that these exhibits were seen by around seven million visitors, rivaling the attendance figures of the previous fairs in London and Paris. This was surprising because Vienna was somewhat distant from the center of European population. Despite the turnout, the Viennese exhibition was a financial disaster; final receipts amounted to only 10 percent of the cost.

Not surprisingly, the exhibits of Bohemian glass firms outnumbered those from all other nations. The display of J. & L. Lobmeyr of Vienna was by far the largest, and it received glowing reviews from the press. Lobmeyr shared its space with the factory of Meyr's Neffe, and the two firms printed a combined catalog of their exhibit which lists the table services shown. These included the famous royal service in the rock crystal style of the 16th and 17th centuries. Ordered by Franz Josef himself, this set is said to have taken three years to complete. It included shapes for every possible table use, decorated with polished engraving of scroll-like tracery, ribbons, and the imperial crest.

Lobmeyr's catalog also lists a table service of bronze and glass designed by Theophil von Hansen and a tankard and goblet with silver mounting designed for the Vienna City Hall (which were shown again in 1876 and 1878). In addition to engraved glass, Lobmeyr showed many examples of enameled glass, including copies of 17th-century *Humpen* in green glass and glasses showing a Near Eastern influence.

The section of the catalog devoted to the Meyr's Neffe exhibit lists primarily colored, cut, and gilded and/or enameled glass. Other Bohemian firms showed the same types of glass.

The French display was disappointing. The only innovative glass was that of P. J. Brocard, who showed his enameled glassware for the first time. This was similar to Lobmeyr's enameled glass with Persian motifs, which was also introduced at this fair. Both manufacturers continued to produce similar glasses through the end of the decade; in fact, there was little change in Brocard's glass for 20 years. Perhaps because this glass so closely resembled Lobmeyr's, it drew little attention from the press.

As usual, cut or engraved colorless glass was predominant in the English exhibits. The most admired piece in these displays was a claret jug engraved by Paul Oppitz, a Bohemian working in England, and shown by W. T. Copeland and Sons. This jug, bought by Sir Richard Wallace before the exhibition closed, is now in the Victoria & Albert Museum. The Birmingham glassmaker Thomas Barnes reported that it took the engraver 213 working days to complete. The *Art-Journal* noted that this jug was without "parallel in the exhibit; it is peerless and alone."

The American display was very small; only two glassmakers are listed in the catalog and both of them made glass signs. Some American pressed glass on view was admired by Barnes, who also noticed "splendid specimens of show glasses for exhibiting seeds and confectionery; also bottles for containing drugs. They are splendid examples of glass blowing, the designs good and the several articles well made."

J. & L. Lobmeyr dominated the Viennese exhibition as Baccarat had the two French fairs. For the first time, the company was able to show the full range of its products to a worldwide audience; its previous exhibits had been much smaller. Lobmeyr's rock crystal designs undoubtedly influenced English production of glass in that style, which became fashionable in the following decade. Innovations at this fair also included the enameled glasses of Brocard and Lobmeyr; these found favor with the public and many were produced. Since the 1850s, the German and Bohemian glass factories had produced copies of their own 17th- and 18th-century glasses. This interest in "historicizing" glassware, fueled by German nationalism, remained strong until the end of the century.

Fig. 10. Claret jug engraved by Paul Oppitz and exhibited ▷ by W. T. Copeland and Sons in Vienna, 1873. H. 28.3 cm. Collection of the Victoria & Albert Museum, London.

Fig. 11. The Art Gallery at the Philadelphia Centennial, 1876,
from *The Centennial Portfolio* by Thompson Westcott.

1876, Philadelphia

In 1869, the Franklin Institute of Philadelphia proposed that an international exhibition in the city's Fairmount Park would be an ideal way to celebrate the centennial of the United States. An Act of Congress, approved in 1871, supported "an International Exhibition of Arts, Manufactures, and Products of the Soil and Mine" to be held in 1876 in celebration of the 100th anniversary of American independence. Congress did not provide any money, but it did permit the sponsors to sell stock so that the American people could finance their own birthday party. W. P. Blake, an American commissioner at the Paris fair in 1867, led a group of delegates to Vienna in 1873 to study that exposition in the hope of avoiding its mistakes.

The Main Exhibition Building (housing manufactures) and Machinery Hall, the largest buildings at the Philadelphia fair, were just inside the main entrance on either side of a square where a fountain designed by Bartholdi had been placed. The Agricultural Building was at the far end of the 236-acre site. The Art Gallery, Horticultural Hall, and 250 smaller buildings were scattered around the park. Despite dissension surrounding the planning, the structures were started on schedule in 1875 and finished by January 1876. President Grant, accompanied by Emperor Dom Pedro of Brazil, opened the exhibition on May 10. The president threw the switch on the mammoth Corliss engine in Machinery Hall and all of the mechanical exhibits roared to life.

One of the fair's most popular attractions was the arm and torch of the Statue of Liberty, which had been placed on view to raise money for the building of a base for the statue. For a small fee, visitors could climb to the balcony around the torch and survey the exhibition. When the exposition closed at the end of October, the exhibits had been seen by nearly 10 million people — a record number and especially remarkable because the population of the United States, 40 million, was much smaller than that of Europe. The fair's gate receipts amounted to less than half of the cost, but city, state, and federal grants covered the deficit. The general feeling was that the American people had enjoyed a truly fine birthday celebration.

Some 130 glass firms exhibited, but the European glass displays were not as numerous as they had been at the previous expositions. Since much European glass was already being sold in America, the manufacturers may have felt no need to expand their markets.

Forty-seven American glassmakers participated, but the glasshouse erected just behind Machinery Hall by the Philadelphia firm of Gillinder & Sons was by far the most popular exhibit. Gillinder, demonstrating great business acumen, built a working factory in which visitors could observe glass being blown, pressed, engraved, and cut. They could also buy souvenirs, which the factory turned out by the thousands. J. S. Ingram's *The Centennial Exposition Described and Illustrated* gave a detailed picture of the operation:

> The whole process of manufacturing glass was here shown, and it was a very interesting and highly instructive exhibit. Many of the articles manufactured were especially designed as me-

mentos of the great exhibition, and found a ready market. These included paper weights, upon which were stamped representations of different Centennial buildings, or public buildings of the city; busts of Washington, Lincoln and others, vases, colored ornaments and trinkets.

For the first time, the American glass manufacturers made an all-out effort. While their works did not earn many accolades from the writers of large art books, they did receive favorable comments in the American press. James D. McCabe's *Illustrated History of the Centennial Exhibition* said:

> The display of glassware along the main aisle was very beautiful and quite extensive. The finest specimens of cut and ground glass were to be seen here. This department extended southward from the main aisle, and embraced also a large collection of plainer and more substantial articles of glass. Wheeling, West Virginia, and Pittsburgh, Pennsylvania, the two principal seats of American glass manufacture, were well represented, and New Jersey and Massachusetts also made superb displays.

The official Belgian report on glass in Philadelphia noted that the lead glass of New England was magnificently represented, adding that the American glass was second in quality only to the Bohemian displays — high praise indeed from a European publication.

The glass exhibits were divided by nation so that the British glass was viewed in the British Department of the Main Building (which housed the manufactures), the Austrian glass was in the Austrian Department, and so forth. The European displays attracted most of the critical attention. *Masterpieces of the Centennial International Exhibition*, one of the "coffee-table books" written about the fair, shows 27 illustrations of glass. Sixteen of the objects shown had been made by J. & L. Lobmeyr, and eight by English firms. On the basis of the pictures, it would seem that Lobmeyr must have sent its 1873 Viennese exhibit nearly intact to Philadelphia. The works illustrated are the same as those shown in the publications for the 1873 fair; indeed, some of the prints are identical. If the objects were from stock, as in many cases they must have been, they were merely pieces of the same design and not necessarily the identical objects. The illustrations show enameled glass in the "Persian" style, engraved glass in the rock crystal style, and other pieces familiar from previous exhibits.

The most impressive British displays were those of James Green and Nephew of London and J. Millar of Edinburgh. Like Lobmeyr, Green showed some of the same glass he had sent to Vienna. A photograph of his exhibit shows traditional colorless cut glass of the type that had been a British specialty since the 18th century.

Surprisingly, the elaborate publications on the Philadelphia exhibition paid little attention to the American glass and much more to Lobmeyr and Green. However, Americans in the 1870s were still afflicted with a sort of national inferiority complex concerning their art, ceramics, and glass. This was the largest display of foreign glass in America since the New York fair of 1853, as well as the first sizable exhibition of American glass anywhere.

For American manufacturers, the fair provided a wonderful opportunity to present their best glass side by side with the European imports, and it is obvious that most of them took full advantage of it. The heavy cut glass shown by the New England Glass Company, by the Boston & Sandwich Glass Company, and especially by Christian Dorflinger's glass company helped to spark a revival of American interest in cut glass which was to culminate in the elaborate brilliant-cut pieces made around the turn of the century. Pressed glass manufacturers from the western states viewed the Philadelphia fair as a chance to attract eastern customers for their cheaper wares. Pressed glass, a mainstay of the American glass industry, was shown in quantity for the first time, and glassmakers who relied on it were eager to show their wares to best advantage.

Fig. 12.   The exhibit of James Green and Nephew of London at ▷ the Philadelphia Centennial Exhibition of 1876. From a stereopticon card in the collection of The Corning Museum of Glass.

Fig. 13.   Facade of the main building for the Paris fair of 1878,
from *L'Exposition de Paris, 1878*.

1878, Paris

France could scarcely afford her scheduled 1878 exposition, but pride demanded that it not be canceled. She was still smarting from defeat in the Franco-Prussian War in 1871, the consequent loss of important territory to Germany, and the political upheavals which followed. The government of the new Third Republic was anxious to convince the world that France was still a major power as well as the European center of art and culture.

A huge rectangular structure was built on the Champs de Mars, and almost everything was housed under one roof. Because the small national buildings had been popular in 1867, the *commissaire-général* invited national governments to erect facades for their sections; these formed a Rue des Nations facing the central courtyard. The building's outer walls were mostly glass interspersed with decorative columns which hid the structural framing.

The exposition was devoted to world peace. This was the first official theme announced for a fair, although promoting world peace had been one of Prince Albert's goals in backing the first international exhibition in 1851. A conference center was erected nearby so that international meetings could take place during the fair. Understandably, there was no German national exhibit; the Franco-Prussian War was too recent for the Germans to be welcome in Paris. The six-month exposition attracted 16 million visitors — a record number.

There were 240 exhibits of glass, nearly two-thirds of which were French, in spite of the fact that the loss of territory to Germany had included several important glass factories, among them the Cristallerie de St. Louis, one of France's largest. Baccarat provided the biggest display. Its most imposing feature was the Temple of Mercury with a silver figure of the god standing at the center. Charles Colné, the American commissioner, described it in detail:

> This temple was constructed with an open cupola of flying spandrels, each a solid curved beam, supported by six handsome Corinthian columns. . . . The base showed a balustrade, upon which . . . were placed six urns. . . . The whole temple was made entirely of glass pieces, cut and adjusted to form the structure. . . . The effect of such a dazzling mass of flint glass was really grand.

Today, the temple is on an island in the middle of an ornamental lake at an estate near Barcelona. At the fair, the temple was surrounded by mirror-topped tables laden with cut and engraved glass which sparkled beneath a dozen or more elaborate chandeliers. Photographs in the Baccarat archives show a glass camel and tables and chairs of cut glass which were also in the Baccarat exhibit.

Not everyone admired Baccarat's glittering display. One French author considered most of the glass illustrated to be old-fashioned, and he characterized the celebrated temple and the glass furniture exhibited by Baccarat and others as ridiculous. Although he admired the work of Brocard, he devoted the largest space to the glass of Emile Gallé of Nancy, who had "abandoned the past for the present, the classical for the picturesque. . . ." The official jury

Fig. 14.   Baccarat exhibit at the Paris fair of 1878. Photograph
courtesy Cristalleries de Baccarat, Paris.

also commended Gallé, whose exhibit must have been small because there is little mention of it in most publications. Only one or two French critics seemed to realize that Gallé, who would become the greatest glassmaker of the late 19th century, was breaking new ground with his enamel work and engraving. Much of his glass was decorated with Near Eastern motifs, but he was also influenced at this time by the arts of Japan. Gallé's father had lost his glass factory in Meisenthal because after the war it was in German territory. As a consequence, he had started a new factory in Nancy which his son was running by 1878.

The Italian displays were dominated by the glassware of the Venice & Murano Glass Company. A large group of glasses illustrated in the *Art-Journal Catalogue* were in the style of Venetian drinking glasses of the 16th and 17th centuries. The more elaborate of these glasses were decorated with flowers, chains, birds, and snakes; they are obviously Victorian even though they were fashioned with earlier techniques. However, there were also enameled glasses which were faithful copies of early Venetian glasses in the Museo Vetraria and the British Museum. Even more remarkable, perhaps, were the replicas of Roman glasses from the Vatican and British Museum collections.

For the first time, English glassmaking was richly represented at a Paris exhibition. Thomas Webb and Company sent a huge display. Not surprisingly, many writers compared the Webb and Baccarat exhibits. They were the two largest glass displays as well as the two Grand Prize winners; each had filled a section with a glittering array of cut and engraved glass. The Webb company's display was much less traditional than Baccarat's. It chose to show a number of newly developed techniques, including the cameo glass recently perfected by John Northwood; this was undoubtedly the most talked-about type in Webb's display. Joseph Leicester, an English glassmaker, described the Milton vase, one of several Northwood pieces on display:

> The spirit displayed in the production of precious work of this kind deserves the highest commendation. The subject is from Milton's Paradise Lost, and represents the coming of Raphael to warn Eve of the danger. . . . The artist has caught the poet's idea, and embodied it in a tangible form. . . . The expression is wonderfully caught and full of earnestness and passion. . . . If you ask yourself what is art, and what it can do, the answer may be found in the effect produced by such work as this.

The 1878 exposition was the first in a decade to have much in the way of innovative glass, which seems to have been the result of a creative explosion. Visitors could see the epitome of traditional 19th-century cut glass in the displays of Webb, Baccarat, and Osler; the historicizing glass of the Venice & Murano Glass Company, Brocard, and J. & L. Lobmeyr; the beginnings of Art Nouveau in Gallé; and the Victorian interpretations of Roman cameo glass which led to the Milton Vase and Portland reproductions. No other fair yielded quite so much in one place.

Fig. 15.   The "Milton Vase," carved by John Northwood from a blank made at Philip Pargeter's Red House Glass Works. H. 33 cm. Collection of Mr. and Mrs. Billy Hitt.

Fig. 16.   Two glasses exhibited by the Venice & Murano Glass Company in Paris in 1878. H. 51.5 cm, 37.8 cm. The Corning Museum of Glass (gifts of the Ruth Bryan Strauss Memorial Foundation).

Fig. 17.   The Eiffel Tower and the 1889 Paris fair, from *L'Exposition de Paris, 1889. Journal hebdomadaire*.

1889, Paris

Having established a practice of holding universal exhibitions on a regular schedule, national pride forced the French government to announce one for 1889, whether the nation could really afford it or not. Officially, the French were celebrating the centennial of the French Revolution, but this was downplayed since some foreign monarchies did not regard the revolution as something to celebrate. Few of the publications about this fair even mention the anniversary of the revolution. There was some initial public opposition to the idea of another expensive fair, but it quickly became apparent that this would be an outstanding exhibition.

From the tourist's standpoint, the most enduring legacy of this fair is the steel structure designed and built for it by Gustave Eiffel. The Eiffel Tower is one of the most photographed and visited places in France and almost everyone in the Western world is familiar with its appearance. Not since the Crystal Palace in 1851 had an exposition building been judged such a technological marvel or attracted so much attention. By the end of March, when the tower was complete, Eiffel escorted a group of dignitaries to the top to hang out the Tricolor. The public, which had complained bitterly about the structure since Eiffel had suggested it, flocked to see Paris from the top. Eiffel, who had personally paid most of the cost of erecting the tower, was able to retain the gate receipts for the first 20 years of its life and to maintain an apartment within it. Before the fair had ended, his expenses had been met, and the next 19 years were all profit.

The other stunning exhibition building was the Galerie des Machines, which roofed an enormous expanse with few interrupting supports. Within the gallery were modern inventions, including Edison's phonograph. This was also the first exhibition to be lighted by electricity; it was impressive during the day but absolutely breathtaking at night when the Eiffel Tower and the fountains were illuminated. The tower and the principal part of the exposition were on the traditional Champs de Mars site. The applied arts were in the Galerie Centrale adjacent to the Galerie des Machines. Nearly 62,000 exhibits were spread over the 237-acre site, and more than 38 million visitors paid to see them. The French government could point with pride to a highly profitable world's fair.

For the first time, United States glassmakers made a real effort to show their wares in Europe. The official catalog of American exhibitors lists 11 displays of glass, including window glass, stained glass by John LaFarge and others, lamp chimneys, and glass signs, as well as a large cut glass exhibit sent by T. G. Hawkes of Corning, New York, who won a Grand Prize.

As in 1878, Thomas Webb and Sons had the largest English glass display, which, on the basis of published descriptions, must have been devoted primarily to cameo glass. Webb also won a Grand Prize.

As far as the French were concerned, Gallé was by far the most important exhibitor, and modern critics probably would agree with that assessment. His glass was shown in the Court of Honor as well as the glass section, and he also had displays in the ceramics and

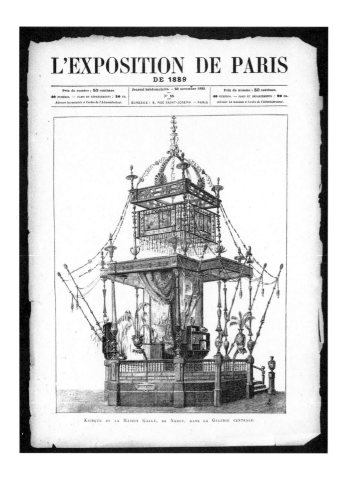

furniture sections. For the Court of Honor, Gallé designed an imposing structure topped by a fanciful vase, with shelves suspended from the balustrade holding vases full of ferns. To modern eyes, the structure looks like something designed for the top of a wedding cake, although the French writer Jules Henrivaux compared it to the tent of a Druid or Gallic chieftain. There could be no greater stylistic contrast than that between Gallé's 1889 "kiosque" and Baccarat's 1878 cut glass temple.

Gallé's glass featured motifs derived from nature, an astonishing repertoire of colors (often combined with engraving), and — most important to the French writers — artistic and poetic sentiments. One writer particularly admired the way Gallé combined colors and motifs in several layers to make "fantasies of charming poetry."

In 1889, Gallé stood alone; no other glassmaker produced works of such complexity or originality. Although he had exhibited at French national expositions, he had not had a worldwide audience before 1889, and his display was to have far-reaching consequences. He was especially influential with French glassmakers, but his ideas spread throughout Europe. Unfortunately, none of his imitators approached his genius.

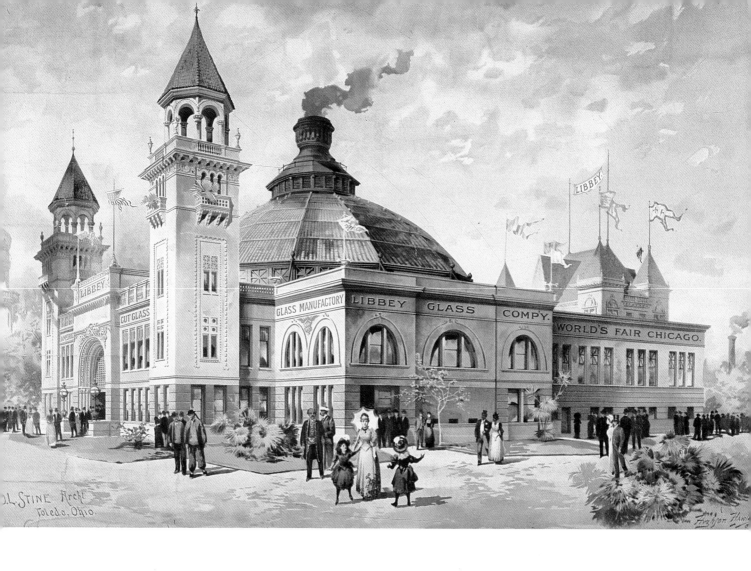

Fig. 20.   Glass factory of the Libbey Glass Company at the Chicago fair of 1893. Courtesy Carl Fauster.

1893, Chicago

After the great success of the nation's 100th birthday party in 1876, there was growing sentiment for a proper celebration in 1892 of the 400th anniversary of the discovery of America by Christopher Columbus. Another international exhibition was the obvious way to mark the occasion, and by 1890 Chicago had been chosen as the location.

The selected site spanned two unfinished city parks: Jackson Park, a swampy area on the edge of Lake Michigan, and Midway Plaisance, a smaller adjacent park. Frederick Law Olmstead, one of the designers of New York's Central Park, planned the 685 acres and brought in tons of landfill to create canals and a central lagoon connected to the lake. Because it was impossible to finish the work on time, the exhibition was "dedicated" late in 1892 and opened in May 1893.

The fair's nickname, the "White City," was inspired by the neo-classical architectural style; white stucco facades were chosen for the eight principal buildings. The main entrance led directly into a large courtyard in front of the Administration Building designed by Richard Morris Hunt. This white building, surmounted by a large golden dome, appeared to be built of stone, but it was actually of wood with imitation stone carving in a form of stucco. Behind this was a large sculptural group showing Columbia on her Ship of State guided by Father Time with Fame on the prow; this mixture of metaphors was typical of the period.

Farther away from the central lagoon were the foreign pavilions and other buildings erected by the federal government and several states. Circling the site was an electric railway, and at the edge of the lake was the famous Movable Sidewalk (also powered by electricity) which allowed visitors to sit on park benches and pass the sights at six miles an hour. For 10 cents, visitors in the Midway Plaisance area could see glass being made at factories built by the Libbey Glass Company of Toledo and the Venice & Murano Glass Company. They could also view "Little Egypt" and other scantily clad native dancers in "The Streets of Cairo." There were Chinese, Tunisian, and several other "national" villages to tour. Fifty cents would buy a ride on a gigantic revolving steel wheel 264 feet in diameter, designed and built by G. W. G. Ferris of Pittsburgh. Ferris's wheel had 36 cars, each of which held 60 passengers. Like Eiffel in Paris, the builder recovered his costs and added a fortune besides. This area of the fair provided a new word for the American vocabulary — Midway — and a new amusement that would grace countless carnivals and county fairs in years to come — the Ferris wheel.

Perhaps the most impressive aspect of the Chicago exposition was the extensive use of electricity, which was still relatively new. The humming engines in Machinery Hall were no longer powered by hissing steam as they had been in London and Philadelphia. Instead, when President Grover Cleveland pressed a gilded telegraph key, he started the Allis engine in the Power House, where 127 dynamos provided the silent power for the entire exhibition. The alternating-current generator displayed by George

Westinghouse, like electric engines and dynamos, was a symbol of the future which was to have great importance for all Americans. Before it closed, the White City had been seen by 27 million visitors.

Most of the more than 70 glass exhibits were in the mammoth Manufactures & Liberal Arts Building. Of the American displays, the Tiffany pavilion won the most praise from the critics, although visitors may have been more appreciative of the Libbey glass factory. European writers, especially, found the work of Louis C. Tiffany's Tiffany Glass and Decorating Company to be among the most admirable exhibits in the White City. The pavilion included two rooms and a chapel. The latter featured several windows with religious themes: "The Entombment," "Christ, Ruler of the Universe," and others. This chapel has been described as Byzantine or Romanesque, but in reality it was Tiffany's own amalgam of stylistic elements. The floor, steps, reredos, altar, font, lectern, and other furniture were all constructed of marble and glass mosaic. This stunning array created much favorable publicity for Tiffany, whose work had been well known only to a limited circle of the wealthy in the East. He was to become the leading American glass designer of the turn of the century, and his windows were nearly as influential in Europe as in the United States.

In one room, Tiffany displayed two more windows, a large composition "Feeding the Flamingoes" and the smaller "Paroquets and Fishbowl." The plumage and water in both of these windows, created in the glass, produce a stunning effect. Tiffany described the latter window as follows:

> In one window there are portrayed a number of paroquets resting upon a branch of a fruit tree in blossom, from which is hanging a globe of gold fishes; the effect produced is most realistic, and has been obtained without the assistance of paints or enamels, solely by using opalescent glass.

Libbey's glass factory was one of the most popular attractions. The *Crockery and Glass Journal* reported:

> The factory at the Fair is a model of completeness. . . . Yesterday a new feature was added to the exhibit which delighted the visitors greatly. Spectators for a small sum each were allowed to "blow" and the funny results . . . kept the great crowds in excellent humor. The cutters and weavers attract most general attention. . . .

The weavers were making fabric from glass threads. Libbey included a glass dress in his display as well as neckties and dolls of fiberglass among his souvenirs. The firm also produced thousands of pressed and blown souvenirs which could be personalized on the spot for visitors.

Like the Philadelphia fair, the White City was principally a showcase for American glass manufacturers. A few European firms exhibited, and those that did sent nothing particularly innovative or exciting. Except for L. C. Tiffany's windows, the glass displayed in Chicago seems to represent a cultural backwater. The splendid Gallé creations shown in Paris had made no impression on American glassmakers. The ideas of Art Nouveau had not yet reached America and the British-inspired Arts and Crafts movement was just beginning. Middle-class America still preferred the familiar cut glass sanctioned by tradition as tasteful; cut glass had represented prestige since the 18th century and fashionable designs in the 1890s were only slightly different from those popular previously. Although Tiffany's widely acclaimed windows were to have a lasting influence on all of the other window manufacturers, their price made them available only to a few. Tiffany's influence today is probably greater than it was in 1893, when his creations were admired by a much smaller group of collectors.

Fig. 21.   Stained glass window exhibited by L. C. Tiffany at the ▷ Chicago fair of 1893. Private collection.

Fig. 22.   The Palace of Electricity and the Castle of Water at the
Paris fair of 1900. Courtesy Bibliothèque Nationale, Paris.

1900, Paris

In the summer of 1892, the French government announced plans to welcome the arrival of the 20th century with an Exposition Universelle bigger and better than any before held. The usual site on the Champs de Mars was extended to include the area of the 1855 Palais de l'Industrie, which was demolished to make room for two new buildings: the Grand Palais and the Petit Palais (both still in use). The Galerie des Machines from the 1889 exhibition was retained. Some of the new buildings followed the prevailing Beaux Arts or academic style, but most of them reflected the popularity of Art Nouveau, which was reaching its peak. The Porte Monumentale, the main entrance to the exposition on the Place de la Concorde, was an elaborate triple-arched structure in Art Nouveau style. Many countries also erected separate pavilions in various architectural styles along the Rue des Nations facing the Seine. To get around the fair, visitors could take the Trottoir Roulant, a moving sidewalk circling the Champs de Mars and the Esplanade des Invalides.

The exposition, spread over the 300-acre site, attracted a record-breaking 48 million visitors to see 80,000 exhibits from more than 40 countries. Despite the tremendous number of visitors, the receipts failed to cover the costs. However, the prestige of holding a popular fair, and of proving to the world once again that their country was a cultural leader, was sufficient compensation for the French government.

There were about 45 exhibitors of glassware and crystal, a much smaller number than at previous fairs. About one-third of the displays were French,

and another third were German; participation from other countries was very limited.

Gallé was still the undisputed leader of the industry. Although he had created several masterpieces between 1889 and 1900, his techniques and style had not changed.

Tiffany was the only American glass exhibitor of note. He was determined to surpass his artistic rival John LaFarge, who had won a gold medal in 1889, and he succeeded triumphantly. His leaded glass window "The Four Seasons" (now at the Morse Gallery of Art in Florida), topped by an eagle, was shown at the entrance to the United States Pavilion along with the window "Religion Enthroned" by Lamb Studios (now in the Brooklyn Museum). The Tiffany Glass and Decorating Company and Tiffany & Company, the New York jewelry store, shared a display which was full of glass vessels. Tiffany's work was also shown by S. Bing, his European agent. The firm's stained glass windows were not new; most of them had been seen in Europe for at least five years in various exhibits. Bing had arranged a showing of Tiffany's art at London's Grafton Galleries in 1899; he had then displayed many of the items in Paris before the exposition opened.

There is no comprehensive list of the Tiffany objects exhibited at the fair, but there are some clues as to what was included. A window showing the Annunciation and another with magnolias were illustrated in an article in *Deutsche Kunst und Dekoration*. A Tiffany Studios brochure indicates that there was also a magnolias window designed by Agnes Northrop, a

Tiffany employee. Other German and French publications show vases, kerosene lamps, plates, and bowls, all in iridescent glass and some with elaborate decoration. The centerpiece of the display was a magnificent golden iridescent glass punch bowl in a metal frame with applied glass jewels. It is illustrated in one article and can be seen in a photograph of the Tiffany exhibit. The work was described as "about 30 inches in diameter. The glass is enclosed in a frame of chased and wrought golden metal. . . . Three of the supports end in quaintly twisted finials of lustre glass from which hang ladles of metal and iridescent glass."

The awarding of prizes in 1900 was astonishing. The glasshouses of Pantin and Sèvres (which produced work heavily influenced by Gallé) received Grand Prizes while Gallé, Tiffany, and Daum Frères were awarded gold medals. Louis C. Tiffany and the director of the Pantin and Sèvres factories were each named Chevalier of the Legion of Honor, a status which Gallé had previously achieved. None of the Bohemian glass firms received medals.

The glass shown in Paris was the ultimate expression of Art Nouveau design in that medium. The fair also afforded visitors an opportunity to study the works of Gallé and Tiffany side by side. The French had planned the exposition to celebrate the end of the 19th century and the beginning of the 20th. It seems a fitting moment for the genius of Gallé to have peaked. Nothing newer, better, or different in glass was to be seen for a quarter of a century.

Fig. 23.   Punch bowl exhibited by L. C. Tiffany at the Paris fair   ▷
of 1900. H. 36.8 cm. Collection of the Virginia Museum of Fine Arts, Lewis Collection (photograph Katherine Wetzel).

Fig. 24. View across the Cascades from German House, from
The World's Fair in Colortypes and Monotones. Courtesy Missouri
Historical Society.

1904, St. Louis

In 1899, a group of Midwesterners decided that a world's fair in 1903 would be an ideal way to commemorate the Louisiana Purchase of 1803, by which President Jefferson at a stroke had more than doubled the size of the infant nation. St. Louis, the largest city within the area of the original purchase, was chosen as the site of the exposition. The organizers raised $15 million from the federal and city governments and from public subscription. The difficulties of planning were such that, like the Chicago fair, the St. Louis exhibition opened one year late. Still, by almost all measurements, it was the largest fair to date. In area, it covered nearly 1,300 acres, more than the Philadelphia and Chicago expositions combined. There were more than 1,500 buildings in all, and the perimeter of the grounds extended for 35 miles. The fair's 70,000 exhibits, which included 34 foreign pavilions, were viewed by nearly 20 million visitors.

The grounds in Forest Park were laid out with terraces, fountains, and cascades. President Theodore Roosevelt pushed the gilded telegraph key (the same one which had been used to open the Chicago fair) in the White House on April 30, and his message declaring the exhibition open was flashed to St. Louis. The engines were started, and one minute and nine seconds later, water was flowing over the cascades illuminated by thousands of lights.

Education was the official theme of the fair, which was supposed to be less of a showcase for manufacturers than previous expositions had been. In spite of this new emphasis, various wonders of technology were on display, including 160 automobiles powered by gasoline, electricity, and steam. Messages could be sent from one side of Forest Park to the other by the new wireless telegraph. A prize of $100,000 awaited the winner of a design competition for the most innovative and successful flying machine, and visitors flocked to the Aeronautics Field to see all the airships, gliders, and balloons. Nothing as solidly memorable as the Ferris wheel was displayed in St. Louis, but the ice cream cone — developed by one of the concessionaires when his ice cream threatened to melt in the summer heat — remains a popular legacy of the 1904 exposition.

For the first time at a world's fair, there was an Applied Arts Section as part of the Fine Arts Department. This was largely a result of the Arts and Crafts movement in the United States, and many of the objects displayed in the new section were the work of individual craftsmen, chosen by regional Arts and Crafts Societies in the United States and England. About two dozen American and European glass displays were included in this area, and around 55 more glass exhibits were housed with other manufactures in the Varied Industries Building.

A collective display of French craftsmen included glass by Gallé and other French artists. Daum Frères, a Nancy factory which was much influenced by Gallé, and the factories of Saint Denis and Pantin each had an exhibit with the other French manufacturers. Gallé's display in the Applied Arts Section contained 24 glass pieces, an inlaid cabinet, a "small piece of drawing room furniture, The Iris," and a rosewood and bronze "Vitis Vinifera" glass case. Gallé had reached his mature style before 1900, and his glass shown in St. Louis was similar to that presented in Paris four years earlier. (Gallé was ill, and this may also have contributed to the lack of new designs from him. He died that September.)

It is somewhat surprising that there were not more American glass companies represented at the St. Louis exposition. The first edition of the *Official Catalogue of Exhibitors* lists only seven, all makers of commercial glassware. The Libbey Glass Company and the Quaker City Cut Glass Company had extensive cut glass exhibits in the Varied Industries Building, and both firms received Grand Prizes.

The Libbey cut glass display is well documented in photographs. It was part of the "Golden Pavilion" of the St. Louis jewelry firm Mermod and Jaccard, which was Libbey's agent in that city. The display is described in the trade paper *China, Glass and Lamps* as follows:

> The cut glass table turned out by the Libbey Glass Co. . . . is 24 inches and represents a cash value of $ 2,500. The cutting required fourteen weeks and is a marvel of artistic detail. . . . it will be outshadowed by another gigantic bowl 24 inches in diameter and worth $ 2,500. . . . The entire exhibit will consist of 1,800 pieces and the cash value is about $ 25,000. . . . It will be a wonderful display and will doubtless compare favorably with the glass cutting exhibits from other nations.

The table and large punch bowl, which remained in the collection of the Libbey firm for many years, are now owned by The Toledo Museum of Art. Libbey also exhibited a large table service with polished engraving, a plaque engraved with the "Apotheosis of Transportation" copied from the doors of Louis Sullivan's Transportation Building for the Chicago fair, and a copy of a large punch bowl the company had presented to President McKinley in 1898.

Twenty Grand Prizes for glass were awarded, a much larger number than at previous fairs. Daum Frères and the Cristallerie de Pantin were among the winners. China's Imperial Institute and one Hungarian firm also received Grand Prizes for glass.

It cannot be said that any of the glass shown in St. Louis was new in concept or design. The English Arts and Crafts glass, which was new to the United States, had not been shown at a world's fair previously, although it had been in production for several years. The cut glass pieces may have been larger than those exhibited in Chicago, but they were stylistically unchanged. However, since the displays of European glass in Chicago had been small, the St. Louis fair offered the first large display of Art Nouveau glass pieces in America; these objects probably had some effect on later production. It was not until the 1925 exhibit of modern decorative arts in Paris that striking changes in glass design became evident.

Fig. 25. Cut glass punch bowl made by the Libbey Glass Company, Toledo, Ohio, for display at the St. Louis world's fair. This was one of the largest punch bowls ever made. D. 63.5 cm. Collection of The Toledo Museum of Art, gift of Owens-Illinois, Inc.

Summary

Looking over the glass shown in this 53-year span, the most obvious conclusion is that innovation was less common than tradition at most of the fairs. Some manufacturers — Baccarat, Apsley Pellatt, Thomas Webb, J. & L. Lobmeyr, and others — never stopped producing heavy cut glass and fine engraved glass. Styles changed and cut glass became less popular during the third quarter of the 19th century, but glassmakers continued to create gigantic "exhibition pieces" in hopes of capturing the public's fancy. Bohemian firms, as well as Venetian ones, persisted in duplicating the same historic glass styles throughout the second half of the century. It is evident from the published artisans' reports that British and Continental craftsmen examined each other's work closely. The craftsmen were interested in methods of manufacture and comparative skills, while the factory owners wished to copy the latest patterns and styles of their competitors.

Juries at the expositions were usually made up of representatives of manufacturers whose firms exhibited but usually did not compete for prizes, because of the obvious conflict of interest. Jurors were inclined to present awards to the showiest exhibits and to glass firms making goods in popular styles. The jury in 1878 gave the innovative Gallé a bronze medal for his enameled and engraved glassware and a Grand Prize to the "traditional" display of Baccarat. Gallé received a Grand Prize at the next fair in 1889. By that time, however, he was much better known, and the jury was confirming the tastes of the cultural avant-garde.

Since glassmakers such as T. G. Hawkes and L. C. Tiffany usually mentioned their awards in their advertisements, it is likely that winning prizes was one of the exhibitors' goals. However, the primary objective must have been the search for new customers. The fairs stimulated international trade in fine glassware by showcasing new designs.

The buildings for the fairs, especially the Crystal Palace, pioneered new uses for glass in architecture and new methods of building which had tremendous influence in their own day. Their legacy can be seen in the glass facades of many of today's buildings. There is even a replica of the 1851 Crystal Palace — the InfoMart in Dallas, Texas — which is larger than the original.

The second half of the 19th century was an era of tremendous technological change in glass, involving experimentation with new formulas, new furnaces, and complicated decorating techniques. Glass manufacturers showed off these developments at the fairs, making the finest glass possible regardless of cost or of the labor it entailed. Visitors could see stunning creations such as the Crystal Fountain and Baccarat's temple. They could look at the glass candelabrum purchased by Queen Victoria in 1851 or the glass dress bought by Princess Eulalia of Spain in 1893, and they could buy the latest in glass for their own homes.

The glass at the fairs was thus the ultimate expression of 19th-century style and taste in this medium. The fairs were a fitting symbol of a grandiose life style which was swept away forever in 1914.

Bibliography

Suggestions for Further Reading

GENERAL

Allwood, John.
  The Great Exhibitions.
  London: Studio Vista, 1977.

Mundt, Barbara.
  *Historismus: Kunstgewerbe zwischen Biedermeier und
  Jugendstil.*
  München: Keyser, 1981.

[Union Centrale des Arts Décoratifs].
  *Le Livre des expositions universelles,
  1851—1989* [sic].
  Paris: Edition des Arts Décoratifs-Herscher,
  1983.

LONDON 1851

The Art Journal.
  *The Art Journal Illustrated Catalogue [of] the Industry
  of All Nations, 1851.*
  London: George Virtue, 1851.

PARIS 1855

[The Art Journal].
  The Exhibition of Art-Industry in Paris, 1855.
  London: George Virtue; Paris: Stassin & Xavier,
  1855.

LONDON 1862

[The Art Journal].
  Catalogue of the International Exhibition 1862.
  London; New York: Virtue, [1862?].

PARIS 1867

The Art Journal.
  The Illustrated Catalogue of the Universal Exhibition.
  London; New York: Virtue, [1868].

United States. Commission to the Paris Exhibition,
  1867.
  *Reports of the United States Commissioners to the
  Paris Universal Exposition, 1867.* Edited by
  William P. Blake. (6 vols.)
  Washington, D. C.: Government Printing
  Office, 1870.

VIENNA 1873

United States. Commission to the Vienna
  International Exhibition of 1873.
  Official Catalogue of the American Department.
  Edited by E. Brewer.
  London: J. M. Johnson & Son, 1873.

PHILADELPHIA 1876

Maass, John.
The Glorious Enterprise: The Centennial Exhibition of 1876 and H. J. Schwarzmann, Architect-in-Chief.
Watkins Glen, N. Y.: American Life Foundation, 1973.

McCabe, James D.
Illustrated History of the Centennial Exhibition.
[1876]. Reprint. Philadelphia;
Chicago: National Publishing Co., [1975].

Smith, Walter.
The Masterpieces of the Centennial International Exhibition Illustrated. Vol. II. Industrial Art.
Philadelphia: Gebbie & Barrie, [1876—1878].

PARIS 1878

The Art Journal.
Illustrated Catalogue of the Paris International Exhibition. 1878.
London: Virtue & Co.; New York: Appleton, 1878.

Colné, Charles.
"Glass and Glassware," in
Reports of the U. S. Commissioner to the Paris Universal Exposition of 1878. (5 vols.)
Washington, D. C.: Government Printing Office, 1888, vol. 3, pp. 227—387.

PARIS 1889

Henrivaux, Jules.
"La Verrerie à l'Exposition Universelle de 1889."
Revue des arts décoratifs.
Vol. 10, no. 6, Dec. 1889, pp. [169]—185.

Marx, Roger.
"La Verrerie."
L'Exposition de Paris de 1889: Journal hebdomadaire.
No. 55, Nov. 23, 1889, pp. 114-115; no. 56, Nov. 30, 1889, pp. 122—123.

CHICAGO 1893

Badger, R. Reid.
The Great American Fair: The World's Columbian Exhibition and American Culture.
Chicago: Nelson Hall, 1979.

Bancroft, H. H.
The Book of the Fair. (2 vols.)
Chicago; San Francisco: Bancroft, 1894.

PARIS 1900

Day, Lewis F.
"The Glass at Paris," in
The Art Journal: The Paris Exhibition 1900.
London: H. Virtue and Co., 1901, pp. 265—270.

Mandell, Richard D.
Paris 1900: The Great World's Fair.
Toronto: University of Toronto Press, 1967.

ST. LOUIS 1904

Fauster, Carl U.
"Libbey Cut Glass Exhibit: St. Louis World's Fair 1904."
Journal of Glass Studies.
Vol. 19, 1977, pp. 160—168.

World's Fairs, 1851–1904

(Exhibitions in boldface are discussed in this book.)

1851	**London, England**	**Great Exhibition of the Works of Industry of All Nations**
1853	Dublin, Ireland	Great Industrial Exhibition
1853-1854	New York, USA	World's Fair of the Works of Industry of All Nations
1855	**Paris, France**	**Exposition Universelle**
1862	**London, England**	**International Exhibition of 1862**
1865	Dublin, Ireland	International Exhibition of Arts and Manufactures
1867	**Paris, France**	**Exposition Universelle**
1871	London, England	First Annual International Exhibition
1872	London, England	Second Annual International Exhibition
1873	London, England	Third Annual International Exhibition
1873	**Vienna, Austria**	**Weltausstellung 1873 Wien**
1874	London, England	Fourth Annual International Exhibition
1875	Santiago, Chile	Exposición Internacional de 1875
1876	**Philadelphia, USA**	**Centennial Exhibition**
1877	Cape Town, South Africa	South African International Exhibition
1878	**Paris, France**	**Exposition Universelle**
1879-1880	Sydney, Australia	Sydney International Exhibition
1880-1881	Melbourne, Australia	International Exhibition
1883	Amsterdam, The Netherlands	Internationale Koloniale en Uitvoerhandel Tentoonstelling te Amsterdam
1883	Boston, USA	The American Exhibition of the Products, Arts and Manufactures of Foreign Nations

1883-1884	Calcutta, India	International Exhibition
1884-1885	New Orleans, USA	World's Industrial and Cotton Centennial Exhibition
1885	Antwerp, Belgium	Exposition Universelle d'Anvers
1886	London, England	Colonial and Indian Exhibition
1887	Adelaide, Australia	Jubilee International Exhibition
1888	Barcelona, Spain	Exposición Universal de Barcelona
1888	Brussels, Belgium	Grand Concours International des Sciences et de l'Industrie
1888	Glasgow, Scotland	International Exhibition
1888-1889	Melbourne, Australia	Centennial International Exhibition
1889	**Paris, France**	**Exposition Universelle**
1891	Kingston, Jamaica	International Exhibition
1891-1892	Launceston, Australia	Tasmania International Exhibition
1893	Kimberley, South Africa	South Africa and International Exhibition
1893	**Chicago, USA**	**World's Columbian Exposition**
1894	San Francisco, USA	California Midwinter International Exposition
1894	Antwerp, Belgium	Exposition Internationale d'Anvers
1894-1895	Hobart, Australia	Tasmania International Exhibition
1897	Guatemala City, Guatemala	Exposición Centro-Americana
1897	Brisbane, Australia	Queensland International Exhibition
1897	Brussels, Belgium	Exposition Internationale
1900	**Paris, France**	**Exposition Universelle**
1901	Buffalo, USA	Pan-American Exposition
1901	Glasgow, Scotland	Glasgow International Exhibition
1902	Turin, Italy	Esposizione Internazionale d'Arte Decorativa Moderna
1902-1903	Tonkin (Hanoi), Indo-China	Exposition Française et Internationale
1904	**St. Louis, USA**	**Louisiana Purchase Exposition**

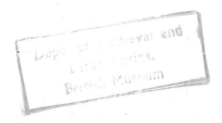

Photo Credits